World Stage Press
Verse from the Village

Yellow
A collection of Poetry and Prose

by Ravina Wadhwani

© 2021 Ravina Wadhwani
YELLOW
ISBN: 978-1-952952-16-6
World Stage Press
First Edition, 2021

All rights reserved. No part of this publication may be reproduced, distributed, or transmitted in any form or by any means, including photocopying, recording, or other electronic or mechanical methods, without the prior written permission of the publisher, except in the case of brief quotations embodied in critical reviews and certain other noncommercial uses permitted by copyright law.

Printed in the United States of America.
Cover Artwork by TMUUN
Layout Design by Fuqi Sun

Yellow is a testament to breaking through darkness to see the sun. Ravina blesses our beings when she shows just how "survival comes before thriving." But she doesn't shy away from the thriving. Her poetry makes you feel that you can hold on another day because the yellow, healing light will be there to kiss your glistening skin and push you forward. You will leave this book asking yourself "when was the last time you thanked your body?" Then, you will go thank it. And live your life in full gratitude.

—Camari Carter Hawkins, author of *Death by Comb*

CONTENTS

INTRODUCTION	17
YELLOW	21

SEEDS

Swallow	25
Soil	29
Songbirds and Bees	33
This is How we Bury Her	35
East & West	37
Grade School Diaries of a Brown Girl with Clipped Wings	41
Child's Play	43
Run Tomboy Run	45
#Girldad	47

STEMS

The Devouring	53
Refuge in your Skin	55
Soothe my Stiff	57
Holy	59
Angels	61
For Gabriel Fernandez and all Other Boys who Have been Failed	63
On Eating Your Spirit Alive	67
The Traveler	69
Deep Fried	71

THE WILTING AND THE BLOOMING

Cycles	75
Stumble	77
Sober	79
No Lifeguard	81
Last Call	83
Nourish	87
The Wind After the Hurricane	91
Broken Enough	93
Mama's Boys	97
Ghost	99
Ride or die	101
Belly ache	103
Morph	105
War Zone	107
Word on the Street	109
Mass Shootings in the United States of America	111
Canvas	113
Tender	117
Tombstone	119
Devil in the Red Stilettos	121
Blaring Loud	123
Lust	127
Be	129
Only Thing Changed was the Block	131
Word Vomit for the Man in my DMs	133
Missed Calls	137

This Country is Caging Our Children	141
The First City That Stole You	143
Hennessy Blues	145
Sink	149
Outro	151

PETALS

On Dying. and Living.	157
Straightened and Scorched	159
Crescent	161
Sip	163
Trust Fall	165
Illusion	167
Spoonful of Honey	171
Barred	173
My Grandmother Before She Became a Grandmother	177
Throat Chakra	179
Sacred	181
Bittersweet	183
The Closing	185
Evolution	187
Twenty-seven	189

POLLEN

Flow	193
The Gift of the Sunflower	195
Spine	197

With a heart overflowing with gratitude to my angel guides in the sky and my angels on Earth, who have chosen to love me in this lifetime.
For the women, family & chosen family who have held and
protected me & never stopped

ACKNOWLEDGMENTS

There are many people who I have had the highest honor of crossing paths with, who have left me speechless, yet with so many words at the same time. I would not have been able to give birth to this collection without them. They make up the foundation of these pages, of my identity as a poet, the people who breathed life into these words and pages, and who I would not be alive without. These individuals and collectives are the reason this flower bloomed. They are my reasons why.

To **Hiram Simms,** poet-professor extraordinaire & captain of the Community Literature Initiative (cli)que; There is no one like you. Thank you for showing up to Never Speak Long Beach's Open Mic as the feature on September 6th, 2019 and giving me a seat at the Community Literature Initiative family table three days later. Long story short, you are proof to me that the universe has a way of putting you exactly where you need to be at the exact time you need to be. You gave me a chance & saw my potential. You watered my seeds & watched me blossom. There is no gift greater than this.

To **Aim4theHeart, Marisol Ibanez, and Leila Steinberg**-AIM is the artistic church I never knew I needed. When you all welcomed this East Coast transplant into space, you helped me find my family of artists, poets, musicians, and lifelong siblings. Thank you for opening your doors and your arms. I do not have enough words to sum up my gratitude for you hearing my words and loving on my craft & allowing me to be myself with you all. You all are my family. You are proof that community is everything.

To the **entire Community Literature Initiative season 7 cohort:** You all helped me raise this love child of mine in these pages.

Your every piece of feedback, every moment spent together Monday nights, every word of love spoken into my pages is the fabric and heartbeat and backbone of this book affirms that there is no *Yellow* without all of you. You are proof that it just takes a group of like-minded people to make big waves. To see you. To hear you and love you for all that you are.

To **World Stage Press** for giving *Yellow* a home.

To **my East Coast family**, and chosen siblings, thank you for being my glue. My biggest blessings. The loves I know I was destined to meet. You are proof that family is beyond blood.

To **Nooshin Valizadeh**, aka Dr. V, aka the #Artivist, Our story is one for the books. Do you see how the stars aligned us? Picture perfectly. Thank you for being my entrance to my first Los Angeles based open mic which turned into my entrance to CLI & my entrance to my first gig in Long Beach as a feature with the Long Beach Literary Society. There is some magic in the way our paths crossed. Only we know how special this is but best believe I'll always be grateful for the way divine timing blessed our lives You are proof that magic is everywhere if we choose to see it. You are proof that everything is connected.

To the **Never Speak Long Beach** crew: Tommy Domino, Dr. V, Jragonfly Jon, Nerd, ShyyButFly & of course Philosophy who had the audacity to crown me as the Silent Assassin (a lifelong honor). Thank you all for all that you bring to my poetry world.

To **Tommy Domino**: the godfather of *Yellow*. Thank you for the hope you bestowed onto me. I am here because you stand. This book exists because in the foundation of this endeavor stood a man who believed in my, a mentor that has always been there for me, a supreme being of love & light. And ultimately, to our students who we had the honor of teaching and planting the seeds of poetry within them, to pass along the sweet fruits of love that exist in the very essence of poetry.

To all of the women in my life from the ones that raised me to the ones that helped me heal through multiple adversities, and those who will always have a bed to rest my bones in and a warm blanket waiting to make me comfortable. To the women who are the reason for my will power to thrive again. To the women who are my best of friends that continue to give me the best moments of my life. This is proof that sisterhood and feminine energy is all that I have ever needed to piece together the parts of myself that make me myself. I love you all beyond measure.

For my father & my brother. My first guides. My first lessons. A whole foundation.

To my chosen sisters. Always.

To **my mother & my grandmother**. You are my everything. You are my proof that all you need is your Mama's love & your grandmother's kitchen and nothing else matters. These are the women that leave me speechless, but give me reasons to write and things to say, all at the same time.

To spirit & my guides, fallen and alive.

To the many moments that happened *for* me, not *to* me.

                                                        to you. for you. thank you.

When you and I entered this world under the yellow of the sun, we left the wombs of women who experienced our births in very different ways. Some of us were swimming in bellies of women who dreamt of us their entire lives. Other mothers were survivors, bouncing through adversity with one intention in mind:

birthing you.

Many of us were floating in our mama's bellies while she experienced a tornado in the four walls of her home. For some of our mamas, we were unexpected little gifts.

A spark.
A light.
A fear.

We may have come by surprise. Unplanned, maybe a bit early, or maybe a miracle she never thought would manifest. For some, our mothers went through nine months of wishing, waiting with all their might, hoping they were doing all of this right without a roadmap or manual, wanting this little miracle to just come out healthy and happy. Some of us never got a chance to know our mothers because we were given as a gift to be loved by other mothers, or fathers or loved ones or community. For some, our mothers sacrificed their lives and their truths for our births, for us to arrive into this world.

And there you were.

A seed,
birthed into a bloom.

You took your first breath of air

and you shrieked and cried

in the glory of a new life.

You didn't know what came before your arrival in the womb. Perhaps you were reincarnated, or brought here through the physical vessel via spirit. How did this life choose us? How did we get assigned to this story? This legacy? How did we come to our mother's wombs?

Birth is a miracle.

With your birth came a whole new world, a whole new energy: you. (Hear me out. Have you ever truly thought about it?) The mere truth that bodies can create life/that life can birth life/can create the world around us/can nurture life. This right here is so magical and so special to me. I'm often so out of words for it/The labor behind it all/A whole production team waiting for you.

Searching for *you*,
dreaming of *you*,
hoping for *you*,
placing your roots firmly in the soil with wrinkled,
tired but steady hands.

Sometimes when I reflect on the strength of my mother, I want to hug her and hold her. Remind her she is and will always be my miracle worker. How she held me in her for nine months. Took care of herself just for me. How she endured the pain, the turmoil and the anguish to birth me.

Life, breath, noise, love, the ability to create, to live, to be here right now, right here What a miracle no? I mean, really step back and, *wow*. You and I and the gardens around us of people we love. We are constantly learning, unlearning, planting, blooming, growing, flourishing under the yellow of the sun. Shifting, evolving and thriving-It is such a blessing to me to feel so alive.

How your journey has unfolded, only you know. Only you know your pain. Only you know your joy. And if you hold the key to all the memoirs and all of the poems of all of the selves living inside of you, you can unleash them. You came into this world not as a blank slate, but rather a universe full of potential and dear life.

The truth is, we are not our mothers. As much as we may hold love in our hearts or hatred in our bones for our mothers or have rocky relationships or can't live without our mother, the truth is we are not them. We have pieces of them within us, but we grow and we learn and we go through this world in ways that lead us to find purpose, connection, love, and comfort in our own ways. Sometimes we forget to inhale compassion into our systems and remind ourselves that we are the first and last to have this exact moment in our very bodies.

But there is resilience. And community. And me who has your back.

Maybe like me, you too know what it is like to feel and feel and feel, and it never stops. I am born from seeds, have grown tall from my roots, have experienced the blooming, the wilting, the shedding and the flourishing.

Like a sunflower, this book will blossom along with you towards the light of the sun if you water it.

> So here we are.
> Our two worlds somehow colliding.
> My words, in your hands.
> Your heart on my mind.

My art seeping into your world.
Your eyes on my thoughts.
Just when I thought things could not get more magical,
Here we are.

And I'm so grateful we've met.

YELLOW

Yellow is the color of my love. Yellow is the sunflower and the way she grows to kiss the yellow of the sun. Yellow is the paintbrush strokes interwoven into California sunsets. Yellow is the color of my aura. It is the way the sunrise greets me every morning through the dusty glass window. It is a reminder that all that rises also falls and all which falls also rises. Yellow is the color that sits pretty on the horizon. It is the lemony scent of a Sunday. It is the cream in the middle of the cookies that Naani used to eat with her chai, and it is the color of dal served for dinner. Yellow is my mother's turmeric stained fingers. Yellow is the pencil, my first tool of liberation. Yellow is the color of the school bus. Yellow is the light that dissolves darkness. Yellow is the color of the ray of sunshine and ray of sunshine is the meaning of the name I was blessed with. Yellow is soft, yet tough and just a little rough around the edges. Yellow is peace, harmony and love. Yellow is survival. A shade of victory. A blooming. A rebirth. A life.

Seeds

SWALLOW

The way she stumbles across my name is a sin,
as if it leaves a bitter taste in her mouth,
dark enough to spit out
halfway through this devouring.

She sits in front of the classroom
halfway on the desk, facing a room of 15 children
with thirsting eyes looking to hear their names
said just right enough
so that they would pass the test of being heard.

As she goes down the alphabetized roster
of names that do not sound like her own
she comes across unfamiliar territory
marked by rivers of East Indian soil,
drenching the very paper in front of her.

Likely, this one is mine.

I know it from the way her eyebrows furrow,
as she hesitates to cross these trenches.
When she gets to the second syllable of my last name
it is as if this formation of valleys and mountains
that exist in the very blueprint of my name
was just a little too wide for her to cross.

And the second the violence starts, a butchering of sorts,
an endless echo of stutters,
an array of uncertainty in her voice.
It is then that I can sense the body language

of my grandmother's grandmother
to be that of a wilting rose.

a letdown, a suffocation,
a compression of an entire anthology of worth
thrown out of the window like a piece of litter.

When she belittles my history by substituting the spice
for a flavor that is a little more familiar,
she finds what is convenient for her
 and swallows it.

It is then that I can hear the army of my ancestors
lining up strategically to fight this violence
to protect my heart from its very first heartbreak.
As she shrinks my name to fit the ridges of her tongue,

one that has never tasted letters
seasoned with cumin, cinnamon, and cloves all at once,
names that remind her that we exist,
names that remind her
of the ugliness of her own ancestors' truths,
names that are oceans of sounds that melt together
in a brown, earthy, mixture of clay, soil and stardust.

Names like ours require a roll of the tongue,
a licking of the lips,
an effort as strong as the women's hands
that carefully crafted these vowels and consonants for me.

Woven together in my name
is the very essence of my grandmother's scent,
the very wrinkles in her wise hands,

the very brown skin that fills our homes
with laughter, stories and circles of women
coming together hand in hand
to carefully stitch together a mosaic of letters
that make up the roadmap.

Women who took their time
to ensure that my name would be my armor.

So, when you stumble across my syllables,
tripping over the fruit that falls from the branches
and you race across the curves way past the speed limit
pushing aside these roadblocks that arise.
When you sound out my name, remember that there is an army
of a matriarchy ready to remind you that
our names were never crafted to sit pretty on your tongue,
never meant to be digested so easily.

But rather, our names are meant to simmer
in the back of your throat
until you realize that what you let marinate on your tongue
for just a few seconds is nothing short
of a truth too flavorful for you to swallow.

SOIL

(for all Brown mamas raising seeds in unfamiliar soil)

My mother was born from the Earth.
She came out with her hands reaching above the soil
grasping for air. Survival.

And when my mother birthed me,
she birthed the revolution that is herself, myself,
and the women before us both.

My mother's hands are tired
rolling out rotis at home while
rocks are thrown at her window.
The sound of chaos had been normal for her.

Go home, they yell. and I have the urge to protect her
with my entire body to tell them,

My mother is home
and the earth knows it too.

My mother taught me that survival often comes before thriving,
and that our existence here is a paradox.
My mother has tears in her eyes when she looks at me.
She realizes in these moments
that though this American dream has been shot down,
blood staining the Earth,
the same place we come from,
that we are home
no matter how infiltrated this soil may be.

She sees me and weeps.
She realizes it was never about a false narrative
with an empty promise
in a land built on the backs of women
who looked like herself.

My mother is a miracle.
What I am or what I became
was something sprouted from her foundation.
My mother was laying down bricks without knowing it.

She built a home within her voice,
a safety net in her scent,
fostering a dream in her lap.
I do not know what to tell my mother
when she tells me she is proud,
when she sees what she could have been
had she not been given to the disposal of others.

Her life was laid out to her like a storyline
as soon as she was given breath, scripted
a series of episodes already narrated for her.
A final draft.

My mother is sick from the words she has swallowed in this lifetime.
My mother was told she was a manufacturer
before she was told she was a movement,
told that she was born to be a mother,
before she was told she was a universe.
My mother cries for the multiple selves within her that died
and she cries when she sees them rebirthed in me.

My mother is a platform.
My mother is exhausted.
She grabs a glass of red wine with one hand
and guilt in the other.

She finds a safe space in me.
Stories of things unsaid
coming out from her stomach up in her throat
and out of her body like freedom.

She carves a narrative into my back.
Etched into my very bones
and that which I can be
is that which she could have been.

My mother tells me I must break free.
She tells me I must show my skin.
We have been silent for too long.
My mother is pissed.

She tells me I must do my thing, tells me I must love fiercely,
but never to give my whole self away.

My mother invested a treasure in me.
A seed growing, grown, blossoming.

So, when I walk down the street and the hollering starts,
chewed tobacco spit onto the sidewalk,
they say *Sweetheart*.
It is then that I remember the swords I carry in my tongue.
It is then that I remember I was born with a waist of knives.
"*Do not touch me*", I tell them,

pepper spraying them with my voice.

As I hide the truth from her,
she finds a way to reel it out of my body like a rope.
She tells me my truth is stronger and fiercer
and louder than the hands of any man who I have survived.
And as her truth stays marinating beneath her tongue,
she tells me to free mine.

I wonder if my mother lives vicariously
through the moments I never tell her about.
Mothers like mine live out their dreams through our hands

as theirs are tied back with rope.

As shattered as I may be from picking up the broken pieces of love
that break on my floor,
I must remember that these cuts and bruises and wounds
are nothing compared to
the first time my mother had to bury her life
before her very own eyes.

SONGBIRDS & BEES

Model minority child sits in a classroom chair,
name plastered onto the wooden desk
right at the front of the room,
eyes burning through the green chalkboard.
Pay attention.

Backpack heavy and loaded with outside expectations
with perfectly sharpened pencils he might use
to carve his way out from this hole.
His father sidewalk chalks his model minority child's name
across finish lines he has yet to cross.
Keep going.

Model minority child sits at the intersection
of reality and expectation,
armed with rage and rebellion.

Spelling bees buzzing around like flies,
pressure building into his backbone.

Instead of letting the bones break, they tell him:

Sit straight
Stand tall
Let us mold you
Hide the emotions
They will not give you acceptance letters for emotions.
Fold the parts of your authentic self into a box (neatly) and shove
them in the drawers.
Are you crying? Stop crying.

Are you failing? Stop failing.
Are you sick? Swallow your words.
Are you hurt? Stick the band aid on yourself.

When I birth my model minority child,
they will explode out of this mold like sweet, sweet revenge.
And they will hold, hand in hand,
those who were forced to suffocate while breathing,
expected to sit still while itching to set themselves free.

and when model minority women
birth model minority children,
we birth a flock of songbirds ready to sing,
scream, kick, shove, and set ablaze the scripts
that they never auditioned for in the first place.

THIS IS HOW WE BURY HER

1. Tell her to close her legs
   as she enters the home of familiar faces.
   Tell her to sit upright. Spine aligned perfectly,
   bones sitting pretty, one under the other.
   Tell her to quietly swallow her voice,
   hide the tears that burst at the seams of her pain.

2. Tell her that her skirt must fall below her knees.
   That she is not entitled to the curves of her own body.
   Tell her to straighten out the speedbumps.
   Strip her of her innocence.
   Tell her to use her hands to write papers
   and to use them to shave, tuck, fold, stir,
   clench, hold, shake hands.
   Tell her to hold trauma in her fingers that is not hers.

3. Tell her that her mind is not enough.
   If her body cannot fit and if her nose is too round
   that means she is not enough.
   Tell her that her growing body is asking for too much.
   Tell her that her stomach is growling too hard.
   One plate is enough

4. Take her voice away,
   then ask her why she gives you her silence.
   Take her choice away,
   then ask her why she did not mention anything about it.
   Tell her she is growing up too fast,
   Ask her to cover up her femininity
   when it is pouncing out of her skin.
   Tell her she is merely a chapter but expect the whole book.

Tell her she must make room,
then ask her why she does not take up space.
Ask her to hold, suck and tuck it in
and ask her why she forgets to breathe.
Put her through a tornado
and ask her why her hair is so unkept.
Give her your burden and ask her why she hasn't slept,
Tell her to cross bridges she isn't ready for
and ask her why her knees turn weak.

5. Draft her to serve food to your guests
and then to serve herself last.
Ask her why she runs through nightmares
when she should be floating in clouds.
Find a flaw and multiply it times 7.
Serve it back to her with a side of self-blame.
Sense the rebel in her smirk and shut that shit down.
Scan her whole body with your eyes when she does not ask.
Tell her to hide, but show her off like a prize when she reeks
of accomplishment. Tell her to fill her cup with *your* dreams
and refine, readjust, and realign hers to fit the gaping holes
that exist in your narratives.

6. Watch as she withers and folds into the fetal position.
See how she crumbles to dust.
Watch how they spread her ashes across oceans.
and have the audacity to ask her to swim.

EAST & WEST

I am of turquoise clear waters of island territory
nestled in West Indies by way of sacrifice from the East.
Bedazzled in my blood is the wisdom of my mothers and grand-
mothers,
and the lessons from protective fathers and grandfathers
who took on the responsibility of providing for their families,
a weight so big you can still see the wear and tear on their
hunched shoulders.

Before I arrived, or was even conceived,
I was already dreamt up
to wear this American dream like a sweater
I am multiple flavors, spices and textures.
I am where kenip meets mango, where East meets West,
where patte', meets mama's homemade curry
I am from kitchens with scents of garlic, onion, ginger and tomato
where East Indian roti meets West Indian roti,
the one we get in the food fairs at carnival
and in the food stands at Holi.

I am from where leaving home
meant being greeted by one dialect,
only to come home to other colloquialisms
and slang woven throughout my childhood.

I am where tomboy and youngest daughter meet.
playing basketball and roughing up my knees while
listening to BET's Top 10 hits and Disney tunes
Celine Dion playing after a round of classical Bollywood tunes,
a soundtrack of stories of my mama's younger life

after Oprah's special on the TV at 4:00 pm.

I am where exotification and oppression meet
lineage of multiple types of colonization.
I am from two histories found in scraps,
in whitewashed curriculums.

Too outsider for home
and too other to fit in on the outside,
but still loved by both.

I am the ghosts of 3 different accents
an eight-minute answer to
"Where are you from?"

I am the child of multiple stamps on passports,
crossing seas to see family
overlooking oceans on planes at age 3,
colors that blur together like diaspora blues.

I am where feathered costumes meet glittered saris.
I am where bindis meet Cruzan hooks.
As tunes of Soca blast from the cars
speeding down streets that look like one ways,
where neighbors greeting "Good Mahnin!" was the standard, and
dirty looks were given out like freebies
if you didn't say it right back

I am doused in an essence of complicated.
I know not what it means to be otherwise.
I am already dreaming of weddings that will feel like a tug of war.
I am already having conversations with my unborn children

about the mosaic of their identity.

I am the lineage and history of paper chasing,
turned into the greatest migration story
birthed from an arranged marriage
raised in a village where palm trees
and white sands were my first home.
and where two parents kept their accents,
while also assimilating to two more.
I am of home where hints of Hindi
were sprinkled into English,
while Daadi taught me to speak another language,
and uncle and aunty infused yet another.

I am from Sunday pizza dinners,
while watching Indian soap operas.

I am two sections of the Ethnic aisles in the supermarket.
school lunches with too much flavor.

I am not easy to digest.
I know I am an anthology
painted with hues of Indian oranges
and shades of Caribbean blue.
But in what other lifetime would I be able
to inhale these many colors?
Have the privilege of being this confused?
This much in constant learning?

---

*Cruzan Hooks; (n) traditionally worn bracelet in the U.S. Virgin Islands *" Daadi" ; (n) grandmother

DIARIES OF A BROWN GIRL WITH CLIPPED WINGS

In second grade, my mom's homemade chicken biryani awaits me in my lunchbox. The sun is blistering and I am hungry as hell. My scrawny little legs find their way to the picnic table. When I unlock the densely spiced, twice recycled container, the girl with the PB&J gives me the eyes. Those eyes. Then proceeds to scrunch up her nose, telling me I should take "whatever *that is*" back to my mom. There is no place for my brownness at the table. This was my earliest recollection of being othered.

In the third grade, my brown name was mispronounced 4 and a half times by the sub in the span of one month and every single time, eyes burned into the back of my head. I was the second to last name on the roster. A mispronunciation followed by my friend Elsia's last name being Williams. I was relieved hers followed mine. It is a reminder that I spent most of my childhood never wanting to be seen or heard for who I was.

In the eighth grade, Aunty G from down the street tells me that I should never NOT get my eyebrows and upper lip done. The first time after the salon waxed it off too thin, I nearly cried. 10 years later, bushy undone eyebrows became trendy, and the little girl in me pre-threading, waxing, and pre-glam is found resurrected from the grave to yet again, accept what was never accepted for me.

In the ninth grade, my best friend Samantha announces she is moving. I mourn the only other brown girl moving who had the same body hair. A girl with curves, and confidence, and a laughter that rippled across the room. I am both sad and okay at the same time. I remember how proud I am jealous but how proud I am of how confident she was in her brown skin. Maybe this will rub off on me one day.

In *10th* grade, in the locker room, I notice how dark the hair on my forearms were compared to Kate's. I wore long sleeves to nearly the rest of the year's classes. It is 90 degrees in the U.S. Virgin Islands. My mom asks me why I cover up and dress like this. I do not have the answer.

In *12th* grade, my first love kisses me under moonlight on the docks. It is 3 a. m. and our friends have left us eight missed calls to ask us our whereabouts, but we do not answer. We are lost in one another's skin. I feel seen. I must have learned to love wildly from him. This was the first boy who loved my brown skin as if it were gold. He tells me that I should shave a little more. I remember why I am shy at the root all over again. I remember being seen as brown and hairy and not perfect all over again.

When I graduated high school, they asked me why I was so calm, why I did not worry about leaving my childhood behind. Truth is, I had been ready for years to be rebirthed into a different life. One where a brown, imperfect woman would be celebrated. Somewhere new. This is how I grew my wings and left the nest. To finally be seen. To finally love myself.

Somewhere in the previous life, the little girl in me is finally crying out with joy. I can feel her on the sunniest of days. I embrace her. I love her wildly. Give her the life she always deserved. The love that doesn't have conditions anymore.

I unclip her wings when no one is watching.

CHILD'S PLAY

Mom always said to pick up the building blocks
all the puzzle pieces and crayons
when I was finished playing

Teacher tells me,
Leave this place better than you found it.
Clean up the mess from the rug.

Put things back where you found them.
Leave it clean for the next person to play with it.
Put it back in its box neatly.

Dad always called me "butterfingers",
said I had a loose grip,
fingers were always trembling.

Don't touch it, they say.
Because *if you touch it you'll break it*
and *if you break it, you buy it.*

And you don't want to pay for something you're not ready to keep,
not ready to hold onto yet.

Maybe this is why love slips through my fingers
before I can grip onto it hard enough,
before I can feel it cut my hands

Maybe this is why I will always stay to pick up the pieces
even when the mess wasn't mine put it back where it came from
gently.

This is why I couldn't break a heart if I tried.
If I did, I'd still give it back to you clean,
still offer you love in these fingertips.

Folded neatly tucked carefully put back into its place.
 for someone else to play with.

RUN TOMBOY RUN

First there was the separation
womb to world in the span of a second,
A shriek and cry, Loss of my first home
and breathing into a new life

Then there were the couple of falls
just to get back up when I learned my own balance.
Falling more times than the rise
was the only way I learned how to walk.
All I needed to get from point A to B
was my own two feet and a will to keep going.

Hurricane Marilyn happened when I was three.
I was taught that all I needed to survive
when the world outside was destroyed, ravaged,
and uneasy to recognize was one candle,
and my father's voice to navigate through the darkness.

The basketball court was the first place where I learned survival.

I had to sweat, run, jump, push my limits,
earn my chance to be seen among the boys around me,
had to prove that I was something to be chosen,
grappling with those who I loved who took up too much space.

But boy could I chase them down the block if I had to.
Thick skin formed from the jump.
How I could still catch my breath when challenged,
broken down, bruised, beaten, yet body still alive.

On the court I wiped my tears on my own,
used my own fingers to rub honey into the wounds of bee stings,
fended for my own damn self,
learned not to take shit from anyone
who grabbed the ball from my hands.

Being the only girl among the boys wasn't a hard thing,
just a constant lesson. My rough edges born
from the fight, from the struggle.
because being the youngest little girl among all of them
meant learning from boys and thinking like them too.

A constant run flip and jump to get to the top.
A continuous chase of claiming my seat at the table.
Shooting a shot for what I wanted and needed.
A dribble and a pass, a rebound from the fight.
A game I have mastered no matter
the scraped knees, cuts and bruises.

Watch me as I run past, to claim what I deserved,
to grasp onto what was meant to be in my hands.

#GIRLDAD

If my father had the language to fully articulate his love for me,
his words would travel to the driest of soils,
in faraway places in the most barren land
filling the void and silence that exists in all the emptiness

Flowers would bloom from his softness.
Gardens would spread like wildfire.
If the world could hear all the ways
in which my father loves me,
there would be tears from the skies,
endless sunshine right after.

I know it because I too lack the words to tell him,
but I will not wait until death does us apart
or takes us together,

My father has lived lifetimes in silence.
My father deserves to know that the love he pours into me,
even in the most silent of ways, speaks volumes.

So, when Kobe went with Gianna,
I wonder if my father thought about us,
thought about how I was just as honored to be his girl
as much as he feels blessed to be a #girldad.

I would want him to know that if we left this world together,
if I were to die in his arms,
if I were never to see beyond the last three minutes,
I would want him to know that he is a world,
That his sacrifices make me love him more,

and that he is not defined solely by his lack of
or what the world never gave him.

That his words,
although sometimes swallowed still reek of love.

Over the phone, before an I love you finds its way across miles of
distance between us, he asks,

"How was work?"
"What did you eat?"
"Did you make it home?"
"When are you visiting?"
"What's for dinner?"
"How is your city?"
"What did you do this weekend?"
"Did you get groceries?"
"Did you eat?"
"Did you eat?"
"Did you eat?"

And I answer:

"When did we learn to swallow the words that we know will set
us free?"
"How is your heart?"
"Do you know you are still my hero?"
"When did phone calls turn into guessing games?"
"When did beating around the bush become easier than sprinting
free?"

My words want to ship themselves over to him.

Some days they find their way out from behind bars,
but on other days they are lost at sea
growing in my throat until they become mountains
too tall for me to see past, to tell him I love him.

My father was the first man to teach me about love languages.
That what is not always put into poetry
doesn't mean that the poems aren't there.

My father taught me that the pride in being a #girldad comes from both ends.

How I wondered what it would be like if it was us in that helicopter.
How there would be some poetic justice
to leaving this world in the arms of a superhero.

Stems

THE DEVOURING

White boy tells me I look "exotic".

So, I ask,
Which serving of fruit or vegetable am I to him today?
What flavor of foreign fruit will I be tonight?

How curious will he be to tighten his grip
on something he has never tasted before?
How soon will he discard the peel like litter?
Will he rush to get to the seed in the middle?
How quickly will he rip through this skin
and pierce his teeth into me?

Juice dripping down his lips, off of his chin.

How soon until he tastes the bruises?
How long will it be before my acid
seeps into the cuts and tears on his fingers and stings?

Will he spit out my seeds?
scatter them across borders of conversations
that my name was never meant to be there in the first place?

Does he not remember that this fruit is already ripe?
Does he not know the bitter taste I will leave in his mouth?

I was never meant to be picked, peeled or cut in half.
I was meant to be pulled back layer by layer.

One   by   one.

Piece by piece.

Not to be devoured in the name of his fetish.
I was meant to be savored,
not swallowed whole.

REFUGE IN YOUR SKIN

There is something so undoubtedly sinful about you/Tell me how you do it? How you make me crumble? I cannot stand it/I have spent lifetimes holding myself together/How you make me lose all of my control in a moment/when I have spent far too many years holding onto every rope and anchor that I could grab on to/I am finally wild when all the rules go away/when you are in my presence/With you, every promise to myself, broken over and over/Every moment, enabling an addiction/How you make me indulge, so willfully without a flinch/so easily/you have me so, so easy/How you make me feel like I am most myself when I hide from all that the world sees me to be/When I am yours for the night/You are my refuge/I am lost and found/a dangerous space to be in/I hate you so much/I love you so much more every time/You are all types of wrong. But everything so right/You are so utterly, indescribably/unapologetically yourself. And it scares me/And I need more/I feen for you on my neediest of nights/You love this/You must love me too/You are my refuge/When you come by, lust drips down my curves like silk, all the way to the floor/Lava/buttons undoing themselves/popping off one by one/like rebellion/skin pressed against other skin/scorch/heat/bodies in synchrony/one movement at a time/a sweet, colorful mosaic of all sensations/a birthright/a gift/bow unwrapped/thrown to the side/Here there is no one else/nothing is in our way/just you, me and the moonlight/and everything is warm again/you know 4 a. m. is my softest spot/Your legs tangle into mine/vines wrapped around one another/Hold me as tonight bleeds into tomorrow and we find ourselves here/In this hour, unphased by the world waiting for us outside/Tell me this is all you need too.

SOOTHE MY STIFF

Heal me with your hands.
Take the night off my shoulders, gently.
Untangle the weight of the afternoon
from the knots in my neck.

Rub the moon into my back.
Close my eyelids slowly and tell me a tale or two.
Whisper ease into my ear.
Take the heaviness off of my spine.

Soothe my chest
as I inhale your frequency
and exhale the bustle of my universe.
Put my trembling hands
in the nest that is your steady palms.

I am tired of building my empire tonight.

Take my ups and downs and put them to the side.
Fold the worries of my tomorrow
and put them in my drawer.
Hold me until I am weightless.

Tuck me into your arms.
Cradle me in your tenderness.
Keep me here until sunrise.

Watch me unfold for tomorrow.
How my creases come undone.
See the wrinkles straighten.

Leave me a little bit softer than yesterday.

HOLY

I was never one to sit still at church,
Never one to feel the vibrations in a room full of prayer.
Not once have I confessed my sins
or sat in front of God in her home.

I found holy in the women that walked their way into my world.
I looked sacred in her big brown eyes and was blessed by her love.

I found holy in the mother on 10th and Redondo,
carrying the weight of a child in each arm,
walking into the obscurity of the night
when there was no bed for them.
Holy is the woman who makes a makeshift bed in her arms.

Holy is the woman who gets out of bed in the morning,
dries tears with the back of her hands,
and continues for survival.

I found holy in the creases of my grandmother's smile,
found godly in the way my mother's tired hands
still put food on the table every night after the day beat her black
and blue.

I found holy in the way my women put their foot down and say
no. I find holy in the ones who strut in with a yes.

Godly is the young girl on the front lines at the protest,
the grandmother with stories weighing down her spine,
the woman who just wants to breathe
but runs marathons each day.
I found holy in the woman who weeps in silence
and puts on a brave face at sunrise,

and who still, still finds a way to dance under moonlight.
I see holy in the way a woman can break and heal
and break and heal in the same day in the same hour.

Holy is the woman who looked depression in the face
and said *not today.*
Holy is the woman who looked heartbreak in the eyes and said
you will not take me this time.

Holy is a mother whose body didn't allow her to become one.
Holy is the survivor, the sister, the daughter
and her soft hands rubbing aloe down her own wounds.
Holy is the voice that sings you to sleep while there is no one to sing to her.

Holy is the woman who asks for nothing in return
and gives everything.

This is my God.

ANGELS
For Joseph Awaida, Raihan Dakhil and their 3-year-old son, Omar who were killed by a driver under the influence of drugs or alcohol in Long Beach Thursday, November 07, 2019.

I imagine they walked into your home after the sun set from this tragedy.

and they must have found
baby's toys sprinkled across the living room floor,
puzzles left unfinished, clothes ready to be folded,
undone dishes, grocery lists on the fridge,
leftovers from aunty's birthday.
sofas stained with the strong scent of your family's love.
A neat room with a half made bed,
ready for someone to rest their bones in it.

A today waiting to turn into a tomorrow.
Life waiting to happen.

We do not pause to think death will come knocking on our doors.
Not today. We do not ever believe it to be true enough
that today may be our last.

You were never supposed to be our reminder
of how fragile all of this is, how none of it matters,
but all of it does at the same time.
Still, we get ready for our sunrises,
our next months, our next years.

How do we mourn those who we can still feel in the air?
Who we can still feel in the streetlights, school buildings,

the places of worship?
When everywhere we turn there you are.

I never believed in heaven or hell
because I never knew the answers,
but tonight, I closed my eyes,
prayed a prayer that resurfaced from a lifetime ago,
lit a candle, hoped that you are reunited up there,
hand in hand, baby's fingers as the bridge connecting mama and
papa, just as you always walked when you roamed your city.

Will you rest in power
knowing that you are alive in the moonshine?
You are everywhere. Still here,
a constant reminder
of what is not promised and what is.

FOR GABRIEL FERNANDEZ & ALL OTHER BOYS WHO HAVE BEEN FAILED

Gabriel Fernandez was an eight-year-old boy whose life was taken from this Earth far before his time. He passed into another realm in May 2013 after being severely abused and tortured by his mother and her boyfriend, both of whom were arrested and convicted for his death.

Dear Gabriel,
If I could find a way to offer you my voice,
to wrap your skin in my words,
heal every broken piece of you with my love.

If I could climb heaven's stairs to tell you
I love you like my own, would you accept this?

Dear Gabriel,
I know an apology could never suffice,
that we cannot make up for the time stolen from you,
the moments we never told you we loved you.

When you needed loving arms around your 8-year-old body,
they gave you wounds.
When you needed a safe soft place to sleep,
they gave you sin.
When you needed a parent, an advocate,
and all that you were born entitled to, they gave you silence.

They turned away, gave you trauma.

Dear Gabriel,
I wish I could have been the one to keep you from leaving the classroom,

wish I could have held you close at the welfare office
or showered you with love on the soccer field.
How I wish we never let you go home because home for you
was just four walls of blades, hatred and a loss of humanity.

How I wish we could let you tell us about your day
and your friends, and the things you dreamt of being.
and hold you and remind you that you are perfect
even when they tried to beat the love out of you.

How you had decades and decades left on this Earth.
How you still loved your mother,
put your heart on your sleeve,
only for it to be removed and taken away from us.
I wonder about the person you deserved to live out to be.

Dear Gabriel,
Would you have been a poet?
Would you have transformed your own pain into gold like us?
Mixed the blues with brighter shades?
Fought for those around you?

How I would have let you just be eight.
How there is no homophobia in the walls
of the home you deserved.
How there are no sharp edges in this home.
No closed doors or nothing that could come close
to tearing through your skin or your spirit.

In my home we learn love, not survival.
In my home we would have cultivated your talents,
loved you for all of you.

How we would have made space
for love to pour out of you like liquid gold.
How we would have let you live.

Dear Gabriel,
Can you hear me?
What is it like up there?
Do you watch over us?
Do you feel safe now?
Can you breathe?

Are you finally free?

ON EATING YOUR SPIRIT ALIVE

How many times have you: eaten at your own spirit?
Gnawed at the parts you hated with your own teeth?
Sunk them into the softest places,
tore the flesh ruthlessly, without hesitation?

How many times have you watered the soil of the ones you love?
Caressed their spirit with your own hands?
Reminded them of their shine?
Rubbed aloe onto their wounds
and left yourself to wither?

How many times have others reminded you of your starlight?
Loved on your spirit even when you didn't believe them?
Even when you couldn't swallow it,
how many times did you purge this love from your system?

How many times have you given yourself permission
to write poems about your own magic
and sealed them in a bottle?
Precious gifts to yourself.
Have you learned to love to the parts you hated
with your own pen?

How many times have you made yourself small?

THE TRAVELER

You didn't pack light.
I know you too well.
You wanted to bring everything
that you held onto in case you needed something.

Love,
leave the baggage at the door.
Here there are no knives, just ears
and arms waiting to hold you
Here, you can choose to keep your shoes on
or leave them at the entrance.
Come bare or come full.

Love,

Do not apologize for your lateness from the long hours of travel.
I know you are worn out from the wrinkles in your forehead
to the creases in your smile.
I know you carry stories in the folds of your fingers.
Here, every scar is celebrated.
I will kiss them one by one and love them anyway.
Every wound treated with honey.
Every inch of your heart, worshipped.
Every ounce of your existence, validated.
Every smirk, laugh, cry, scream, smile, tear, frown, upheld.

Every chapter, every verse, every stanza of yours, a gift to me.
Here, there are no parts that we can do without.
Here, there are two arms to call yours
and a blanket to warm your feet

and a love to hold you close.

You are home no matter the rips in your jeans,
the tears in your skin,
the withering of your voice,
the tired hands and aching feet.

Lay your body to rest and let me lay mine next to yours.

This is your homecoming.

DEEP FRIED

You lure me in with your carefully thought out words
covered in sugar, dipped in cinnamon.
The scent of deep-fried bliss fills my lungs.
This becomes the sweet spot.

A craving I will feel with my tongue.
A burning desire for your syllables
to find their way into my ears,
the vessel being a whisper or two.

The sweet spot becomes the soft spot.
You rub the honey into my skin with your fingers.

My muscles soften,
the tension leaves.
You make your imprint on my heart,
carved with your fingernails.

This is how you never leave, even when you do.
This is how you win my words of praise
in every conversation that your name invades.

In every version of every story of you, of us,
I will always taste the sugar on the rim
instead of the salt.
It will always taste like honey jack,
or a semi-sweet wine,
never the sharp taste of vodka.

It will be like this every time.

How the sweet tooth overshadows the desire for savory.
How the tender moments stay longer in my photographic
memory over every wrongdoing.

I wonder if you consider yourself lucky
that I never regret what I swallowed whole,
chugged straight and never chased with regret,
no matter how much it burned the back of my throat.

How the sweet spot turns soft spot
turns lesson learned.
How you will always be a lesson,
a warning of what not to take in next time.
You are never a source of rage.
You will never be the seething, never the regret.

Just the true taste of bittersweet.

The wilting and the blomming

CYCLES

Take the dirty laundry.
Place it in a pile
piece by piece.
Let it sit for a while.

Watch as it gets bigger.
Notice your avoidance.
Notice your dismissal.
Watch as it grows.

Until it becomes heavy,
a load.

Until you are pushed to take care of it.
As piles of old emotions,
attached to big sweaters,
and memories woven into denim.

Blended into one, an old colorful mess.

You take the load onto your own shoulders.
You find a safe, clean space to dump it all in.
Let it sort itself out–
separate the blues and the grays.

Watch as it swivels, stirs, turns, twists, and winds.

Take out the truth that is soaking wet and raw.
Find a safe space to air it all out.
Let it dry.

Let it heal.

The stains now exposed,
like the old wounds you take with you.

Like a Sunday chore, it becomes repetitive.
The old patterns find their way to mix in
with the new in the next cycle.
Watch as the creases begin to straighten themselves out.
See how a breath of fresh air
dries out all that you once wished to discard or donate.

in the name of healing.

Take the dirty laundry elsewhere,
somewhere where it will not dampen the love
you so deserve.

Fold it gently.
Sort the colors.
Match the pairs that need to be put back together, like pieces of
your history.

Big oversized sweaters
for someone new to wear.

STUMBLE

I will not apologize
for
the
times
I
doused my pain
in
Hennessy.
I needed to
break
over
and over
to fall
back
in place.
I will
not choose
to bury
the weaker,
louder,
messier,
times.
They
only made me
drunkenly
stumble
and
fall
back in
love
with myself.

SOBER

I find remnants of you
scattered across this city
in these streetlights
woven into this pillowcase.

I find doses of you
across the curvy back roads,
shortcuts you taught me
that give me an extra five minutes
to witness the moonlight on the way home.

I find your residue
in the dimly lit corners of local bars,
alleyways, street signs and coffee shop menus.

I do not flinch anymore,
do not tremble at the scents that give me withdrawal symptoms.
There is no more insomnia from reeling over you.

Here, there is only a Mr. Clean magic eraser
to scrub the dirt off the walls,
a wrecking ball to break down the cement,
a renovation of an old empty building.

There is only glitter
spread across all the places where you used to lay.
No more cravings, just a hunger to be held by moonlight.

Here there are no more traces of you,
just a redefinition, a recovery, a detox of my bloodstream.

An anniversary of a year of sobriety.

NO LIFEGUARD

In my version of the story, we reclaim joy as our own. Deny all things that tell us otherwise. We brush the second guessing off our shoulders with style. Lay doubt to rest in its own casket. In my version, we live all of this out LOUD. We say fuck you to the lifeguards. We drown together. Forget tomorrow, we love as if the entire planet will be set ablaze by nightfall. We make sure that every second is a scene, every minute a movie, every hour a sequel. We write our way out of our own suppression. We carve our way out of this hole/Holy. In my version we are as whole as we can be. We love ourselves even more than we love each other because in my version we are so in love and so fed, and so wholesome, that everything else blurs. But we are so present here. In this version in this minute, we cannot stop this flame. In this version, we let it all burn. There is nothing left to lose. We lay all cards on the table. We one up Bonnie and Clyde. We quit our jobs just to hop on trains and love the hell out of each other. That is enough of a two weeks' notice that we need to give out. In this version you do not let me frame my flaws as my flaws. You kiss them each on the forehead and tuck them into bed. Sing lullabies smoothly in my ear. Call me yours/And in this part, my skin becomes yours. There are no barriers in this story. No distance. In this version we don't have a mute button. Our love exists everywhere. We graffiti our truths/Our love is megaphone loud. Blaring, blasting, contagious virus. In this version we are the virus. I won't be able to get enough of you because in this version I won't worry about you leaving. I worry about the shortage of minutes we have together on this Earth. In these bodies. In this version we practice how we will find our way in the next lifetime to each other. You tell me what to yell out in the ether so that you will find me in the next dimension. In this lifetime, we heal. We love so that others find freedom in our story. In this version we are the ones who become liberated. In this version, my layers are never complicated, only worshipped. You untangle them one by one, just how you untangle the knots out of my back. Every past love becomes a spell of gratitude because they made their way out the door for ours to blossom in place of the absence. In this version, you are mine. My largest truth. And this becomes my biggest survival story. My loudest scream/A riot/A reclaiming/A piece of art/alive.

LAST CALL

2 a.m. calls my name,
tells me to find my way home.
"It is late. You must leave."

What will 2 a.m. say when I tell her
that I have grown too used to building walls for shelter
and homes within bodies
and resting my head upon pillows of arms
finding refuge in the skin of those who melt into mine?

What will she say when I tell her
I have grown too used to laying my secrets to rest
in ears that become caskets, in voices that become blankets,
and those who sometimes stay and other times leave?

When 2 a.m. calls, I will tell her,
she is a potent time, but my hands are tired
and my bones ache, as home changes colors and textures
faster than night turns into day

and soon, a new moon comes
and she brings with her a new set of eyes
that become windows.
New skin becomes sustenance,
fresh fingers that intertwine themselves into mine
searching for warmth.

2 a.m. calls my name
and tells me to find my way home
"It is late. You must leave."

I tell her, I am so used to building homes
within memories in corners of fifth floor apartments
in the sounds of the 4 a. m. hollering on the sidewalks
and within the shadows we see dancing around our walls
when the two of us stay awake way past our bedtime.

I am so used to finding shelter
in half cleaned kitchens of cigarette smoke,
empty beer bottles, half open windows
and clothes sprinkled onto the floor,
sunrises that our eyes were never meant to meet.

I have built homes in tongues that taste like regret
and others, the sweet taste of something I deserved.

My homes smell like warm honey until they don't.

Until the door stops buzzing open
or the ringing doesn't stop
and I am sent to the mailbox.

Suddenly, home feels like an empty set of four walls,
an echo, an eviction,
a structure waiting to be occupied,
to relieve itself from its bare silence,

2 a.m. calls and I ask her,

What is home but a lover who doesn't have one themselves?
What is home but skin sticking to one another,
yearning to belong?
What are we all but ghosts searching for homes,

drifting in and out of each other's poems,
stumbling through the hallways into beds
into arms into curves of necks and folds of skin
and joints and bones and soft touches?

Maybe, *just maybe* home is a collection of blueprints,
an empty street with dusty lamp posts.
Maybe home is an empty bed in East Coast winter,
waiting to be warmed.
Maybe home is the curve of your back
when the moonlight gracefully seeps in through the window.

2 a.m. calls my name and asks me to find my way home.
"It is late. You must leave."

I wander yet again, my feet navigating themselves
across sidewalks, curbs and horns.
My body lays itself to rest on sheets with others' names on them.
Soon enough, 2 a.m. begins to fade
with the moon returning to its hiding place
and the sun building its own home in my flesh.

NOURISH

My love is a wildfire,
demanding, orange riot
smoke show, eruption, disruption
shaky, trembling, earthquake.

My love is kind, but needy,
tender and holy,
sacred and fertile.
My love is a brick wall waiting to be smashed
into one million pieces.
My love is a sensitive, summer thing.
My love is you and I,
undressing each other's poems with our voices
caressing each wound in every stanza.

My love is shelter.
My love is abundance.
My love is high standard, but a fast fall
a trip, a drunken stumble,
a knee to concrete scraping perfectly moisturized skin
demanding to go deeper,
curious of what shade will bleed from within you.

My love finds refuge within your veins,
calls you home,
infuses itself in your every inhale and exhale,
calls you everything, calls you at night,
calls you in the morning

My love is seamless reciprocity.

My love gives and gives
and gives and gives
and gives and gives.

Until it is bruised,
and then gives some more.

My love is a mother, a warm, but tired voice
at the other end of the line, incredibly exhausted,
but still puts you to sleep with her cracked hands.
My love is wounded soldier asking to be loved
regardless of losing parts of itself in previous wars.
My love is the knife and the gauze.
the fire and the tsunami,
and the stillness of the lake.
My love is a little extra sugar and cinnamon
in Sunday banana chocolate chip pancakes.
My love overextends and over protects and knows it.
My love keeps you safe even from miles away.
and will keep you up at night.
My love walks boldly into trouble,
survives the quicksand and lives to tell the tale.

My love is the coziest seat at the table
and the unmade beds upstairs.
My love is snowy Sundays stuck inside
with fleece and velvet covers.
A breath, a backbone, and a lullaby
soothes like Vicks, heals like aloe.
My love is paper cut wound,
reminders of what is not easy to sit with,
but worth the read.

My love bleeds,
and bleeds
and bleeds
and bleeds
and bleeds
until dry and still survives.

My love is inside out,
heart on sleeve, beat breaking out of chest.
My love will remind you that you exist,
wringing out stories from within your deepest corners.

My love will support, sting, soothe scream, shout and riot.
My love is untamed, curly hair, kinks and all.
My love is everywhere,
brings you home just by holding it in your arms.

My love is godly, lives in a temple,
comes out when worshipped.

reminds you of a prayer.

THE WIND AFTER THE HURRICANE

I used to be another woman.
I mean, I am her- but just not today.

I feel the withering happen
on the days when none of this makes sense.
when everything evaporates in front of my eyes

I feel the digression
It feels like a shriveling
A condensing into a smaller version of myself

These are the days in which the world is larger,
and I am not.
When I cannot just strut in anymore

When my bones are tired and need to rest
but are called to war over and over again and again
This is how I have lost myself every time

Given more, felt emptier than fulfilled by doing so

Built an empire with scabbed knuckles, and wounded hands
How do you not expect me to bleed?

I have tried and tried and tried
There are some days in which I want to say no
I know how to pick my battles
but these days the battles know how to pick me

Resilience is the thick skin formed after the hurricane
This is what my grandmother told me

But what is it called when the eye of the hurricane still lingers?
When you are stuck in the aftermath of a war you did not ask for?

Who passed this down to me from above?
What is the lesson here?

Depression will remind you that
there is something bigger than you
That you must constantly prove to yourself that you can fight
before it swallows you
before it takes you
Once it finds your skin, depression becomes the constant.
The choosing of a higher road is constant.
The choosing to defeat depression is the constant.
A constant fight.

I am tired of balled fists and unanswered wishes
that were supposed to be manifested by now
I am sick from fighting something I cannot see but can only feel.

Depression will be the opposing force,
the only visitor welcoming you home on your loneliest of days

Somehow the wind will always remind you
that you are alive and will find you
& brush against your cheekbones when you are numb.
It will be the only thing you can feel
when there is nothing left to feel at all.

Earth will catch your fall.
Gravity will bring you back some way or the other
This is the only truth I know
about battling something out in the open like this

BROKEN ENOUGH

When they leave, will you thank them for loving you?
or will you thank them for breaking you open enough to feel again?

When they leave,

allow your stomach to feel the void.
It will happen right away, unwarranted
& it will feel like a tug at your roots of your home
that you built with the very two hands trying to keep it all together.

It will feel empty, shrinking. a freshly dug up pit.
pulled from the roots, back down into the shallows of the Earth
Something taken away from you
& replaced with a bitter taste in your mouth in exchange.

You will not know how to speak in tongue,
but rather through your eyes.
It will feel like pain.

You will replay your credits over and over
and you will justify your role
and you will justify theirs
and you will ask yourself what you did
to deserve to be kicked out of the theater
before the curtain closes.

You did not approve this script.
It will feel like a scene is missing.
When they leave it will feel like the horror genre
and the drama genres

produced a love child.
When they leave you will remember the last time you came home
to two pillars of arms.
You will feel as if you survived something greater than yourself
and had lost something greater than yourself.

When they leave, you will remember the look in their eyes
before the foundation fell.
You will tell yourself lies to make it feel unreal;
It will feel unreal for some time.

Everybody around you will want to love you back to yourself
to feel warmth from being out open
and wounded on the ice for too long

You will resort to feeling the pain instead.
I know it feels safer to be in familiar violence than in silence
In this part, you will be responsible for your own resurrection

You will wipe your face on the subway train
when you pass the places
where your memories come alive
and then wilt before your eyes in the same second.

Places you shared love together in
Coffee shops with the Nutella lattes you'd order
with the extra whip
the corner store you went to at 2 am when you were both drunk
& obnoxiously falling over each other in.
Your favorite take out spot,
The one that made you feel less far from home.
The stop you would get off on the #57 bus

to walk to their home in snowy Boston winter,
with one glove missing, and not enough layers

This will all flash in the same moment
until the train comes to a halt
You will dismiss it as allergies or sickness
when they ask where the light in your face has gone
that everything is ok
It is ok to live this lie only temporarily

So, when they leave, you must lay the remains out on a table
Do not touch them
Let them bleed for a while.
Digest this through your senses.
Let the wounds swell a little before you Vapo Rub them
Unleash your breath
You have been holding it in until blue

Pick up the broken pieces one by one
and place them in a soft place.
Somewhere in the back of your heart.

Give the photos a proper funeral
A burial in the sand
You will write love letters to yourself
Stitch them together into something to take with you

The heartache will mold itself into a lesson learned–
a death, a memorial of what was never yours to hold onto.
This is when your voice and skin,
will begin to feel less foreign again.
and you will welcome yourself on your own doorstep

when your shaky wrists finally twist the knob.

and you will ask yourself again,

When they leave
Will you thank them for loving you?
Or will you thank them for breaking you open enough to feel again?

MAMA'S BOYS

To the mothers of the men I have loved
I do not know how to tell you how sorry I am
that he stole the love you gave him & turned it sour.

I am sorry he forgot all that you taught him
Forgot that he came from a mother
Came from a woman
That his home on this Earth is made possible
by a mother/by a woman
You knew he was always terrible at following directions.

Mamas, don't trip
It was not always your fault he lost the roadmap.
decided to find his way, his own way.
I am sorry that you lost him.

I know you do not recognize the way he let me down
I know you do not say anything because
I know you have felt it before too.

You know of the pain from the way his father held you close,
but not enough
I am sorry that the way you cared for him did not suffice
That he chose to use poison instead of medicine
& sold it to me in the name of affection

I am sorry you had to hear all the details of the story
that you could not recognize him
I am sorry you weep when you find my shambles
when they remind you of a mirror image of your own loss

how you lose new daughters over and over again

Mamas,
The one you raised left the nest
Found new homes to temporarily bury himself into
Deep, 6 feet under sometimes

My guess is he mistook my love for something
that reminded him of yours
& he could not digest it.
I guess he could not handle what his father couldn't either.
Your son turned wolf, turned story,
condensed into poem, reduced to a few lines.

Mamas, find rest now.
Soften your shoulders and your furrowed eyebrows
Quit putting puzzle pieces together that do not fit.
Most importantly Mama,
Do not find more ways to hold him close
when the love you gave him has already left the building.

GHOST

When I see you with her,
same love you hand her with your two hands
that used to hold me
I see a freedom in your eyes
A love, sprouting in your rosy cheeks.

I see the lessons you learned from me mastered.
I wonder how the taste of my love feels on her tongue.

Do you finally comprehend how I will always be in your presence?
Not in my flesh, but in your tongue?
Not in my own body, but in your veins?
A constant reference, an association, a default.

Maybe I will learn to rest when you set everything ablaze,
when you burn me out of your picture fully.

For now, I will rest my hands,
knowing that I still live on
in the curve of your smile
and in the way her smile curves too.

RIDE OR DIE
(for my chosen sisters)

You may not remember the day I wanted to jump out of my own skin,
but it plays over and over in my mind like elevator music.

You breathed life back into me without even knowing it,
took my broken pieces and reminded me of the days
where I was not so torn.

You threw pity out the window and brought in your words,
clothed me with them on the days I felt most vulnerable,
most wounded, most open.
You knew.

I didn't ask.
You didn't push.
You chose the softer route, even in the harshest of nights.
When the world was hard on my shoulders, weighing too heavy.
You recognized the pain.
You had seen it in your own lifetime many times.
You knew.
You reminded me I was a growing thing.
A learning thing, never a broken thing.

You didn't tell me it was going to be okay.
You told me it was going to get better.
You fed me honey when all I could taste was bittersweet,
when all I could hear was shattering, breaking, loud glass,
when all I could see was gray.
You reminded me of my strength.

You knew.

There are days when I cannot name this type of gratitude.
So I do not try. I do not force.
You taught me to be. I let it flow.

For every sister found along the way,
my life is *an endless* I owe you.
You are the love who knows my heart inside and out,
who accepts my every layer without poking, shifting, peeling or probing.

I do not know what language to shower you with
to express to you that my hope is we meet in every lifetime.
For now, I will give you my heart,
Hopefully, it is enough.

BELLY ACHE

When I tell you *I miss you*,
Do you know the ache in my stomach?
An empty hole,
a void that can only be filled by your embrace.

When you tell me you miss me,
do you know of the shrinking in my gut?
It is a pining, a longing, to be held by you,
a feeling I cannot name.
It is a rush to the belly; I can tell you where I feel it,
a hunger starved for too long by this distance.

When I tell you *I miss you*, know that if I could,
I'd swing through vines of constellations,
land on the moon, ask the sun to carry me back to Earth,
so that I can cut through this distance
just to be held, warmed by your arms.

What I would give up right now
to place my head on your chest
right near your heartbeat
to be one with you again.

MORPH

Time and time again there it is.
The thing you avoid,
the thing you do not want to feel anymore
grows new thorns.

It finds its way out from under
after you tried to bury it alive.
It breathes in new air,
spits out new venom,
sprouts out of your own skin from a wound
waiting to be loved, to be healed.

The lesson you do not want to confront
leaves bite marks on your shoulders,
scratches for your attention,
takes off your blind fold.

Until you hold its spikes in the palms of your hands,
until you look it in its eyes,
it will find a way into your safe spaces,
haunting your four walls.

It shows up as an echo sometimes,
and other times a scream,
tugging at your legs like a young child
waiting to be picked up in your arms.

Time will throw you the same blueprint
of the same lesson one more time
until you have mastered it,

then find new ways to present to you the obstacles
you think you cannot defeat, in different cloth

until you have learned to not let it consume you,
but rather let it move you in the right direction.

Healing that big beating thing that is alive in your chest
means letting it bleed a little
until your fingers have the strength again
to rub honey into the muscle
after you remove the swords one by one.

Time will tell you to be intimate with your demons,
not to move closer to them
but to learn the ways
in which you need to move away from them.
How they need to be buried back, not alive
Just a lesson to tuck back into the bookshelf
to show you that what is thrown your way
will not always swallow you whole.

Time will hold your hand.
It will ask you to dissect whatever it is
you are running away from
until you learn to stop inhaling the toxins
that the world is trying to keep you safe from,
the ones that pollute your lungs.

Time brings to you
lessons you did not deserve to learn,
ones you didn't ask for,
and ones you needed
but didn't think you did.

WARZONE

Call me a masochist,
an addict to internal chaos.
I have been at war with myself for a lifetime,
denied myself the fruit I so badly crave,
loosened my grip on all that keeps me afloat.

I operate in a state of turmoil,
when the world around me offers me peace for once.
I have spit out the blessings
that have fallen like snowflakes on my tongue
while praying for them at the same time.
I've loved on the wrong things
and tore up the right ones,
gazed at the beauty of the moon
and selfishly wanted only the sun.

When the world around me came rushing to my doorstep
with love flowers, sugar and everything else sweet,
the kind of tenderness I prayed for,
I keep the shutters down and double locked all the doors.
told others I lost my way when they lit my path for me.

Purged out the good love when it came swimming through my system,
decided to run straight to the bad news,
ignored sweet love with open eyes
while trying to grasp onto it at the same time.

I am a wounded thing,
bruised, battered, recovering thing.

I have been this way since you left.

There are nights where I catch a glimpse of my softness,
a ghost from months past.
As I reach my arms out to hold onto the tender light,
my hands begin to clench, and a fist begins to form.

They say you must chip at the ice piece by piece
to break it down fully.
In this case, I am an iceberg,
a massive roadblock standing in my own way.

When the light enters in tomorrow,
take away the blinds,
force the sun into my skin,
let her kiss me back to life.

WORD ON THE STREET

"Ma'am, my mother went to USC. She got herself a master's degree, but don't nobody believe her. No one. They just don't. My mama got locked up. They took her. She in the psych ward, can you believe? My mama means well. I promise she does. Can you believe that a person in the psych ward holds a master's degree? Do you see how they don't believe her? My mama got a master's degree. A master's degree. My mama is smart. She's a smart woman. But who wants to be so smart that they go insane?"

Who wants to be so smart that
    they go insane?

Who
Wants
To
Be
So
Smart
That they go insane.
                      Who

wants to be pushed to the edge/when alone/because the only people there to break your fall is the state? They will/nurture environments that make the sane lose their minds/and then lock you in a cage/when all you want to do is spread your wings. They will hold you because they will deem you "uncontrollable"/put you in therapy just to/play Tetris in your throat using pills. They will give you a cold hard white room to have space to breathe, but no blankets to keep you warm/as if bare walls could make you find the light at the end of the tunnel. Where are the colors?/They will only allow your family to visit during certain hours. You will only have yourself to love on and sometimes you don't even know how to love on yourself. I wonder if her mama got a Masters in sociology?/I knew the systems that were out to get her. Or maybe the degree was in biology. Maybe she knew what state the body goes into when sent into a shock and starved and fed lies and false hopes. Maybe she knew what was coming. Maybe she didn't. Maybe degrees ain't shit. Maybe degrees can't help you claw your way back out of the casket./Degrees don't make you immune to the oppression now. Maybe mama was just being herself and got trapped because someone did something to her and she couldn't help but to lose her shit./I mean can't we all relate?/Don't love got me doing the same thing every night?/I mean what if her mother was too bold, too much herself that they needed to tame her? couldn't hold herself back/ Ain't this the truth if your skin absorbs the sun? Don't you radiate too much? Ain't that the point of getting a Master's degree? Why don't they believe her?/Why can't they let her sit at the top and enjoy the view?/Why don't they believe that someone of color could shine so bright that our power threatens those who don't see us? Don't they know that woman can turn wolf too? Don't they know we can become master's too? Why don't they believe she got a Master's degree?

Ain't graduation just the beginning?

MASS SHOOTINGS IN THE UNITED STATES OF AMERICA

Nowhere is safe. Nowhere is safe Nowhere is safe. **Nowhere is safe.**

CANVAS

When was the last time you thanked your body?
Your chest, a cage for your beating pulsing core of a heart.
Your body, a home for wisdom,
vessel for ancestral messages coded in your veins.

Your body, a canvas carefully constructed coliseum
home to your life.

When was the last time you thanked your body for surviving you?
For holding you close when someone punched you with their words,
hit you with their heartbreak, pushed you in the dirt
when you didn't deserve to feel weak in the knees?
Your body, catching your fall reminded you to rest,
gave you no other choice.
how your body held the broken pieces of you together as one.

Your thighs, two pillars of strength.
Your feet, that have got you miles and miles through the street
when there was no other way to your lover's home.
Your flesh, living proof of your existence in this world,
your skin, mosaic of truth, memoir, written with red ink.
Your body, loom for all the messages woven into you
from women before you.

How you housed lovers in your arms,
your mother in your heartbeat.
How you itched your way back into your skin to feel again
bleeding along the way.

And the body said, "I will still love you. I will still hold you."

No matter how much you deprived from your body,
your body came back for more.
It stayed thriving through Boston winter,
Fought, and froze to protect you.
It held together when ice tried to pierce the flesh,
Still stayed with you when heat tried to scorn the skin,
How the body wore its heart on its sleeve and still protected you.

When was the last time you thanked your body
for housing your breath?
a home, a place to go in and out, inhale and exhale.
When was the last time you thanked your lungs
for breathing memories into you?
Your stomach, a gallery for all that has made you nervous
and all that has made you full
Your body, home to your hunger and thirst to be loved.
A home to a life, blooming inside of you.
Your body, a garden, someone's refuge,
home of explosive firework, tingling feeling of love.

How lucky we are to love and to break
and to heal in the same suit of bone flesh and blood.

When was the last time you thanked your body?
for inhaling in the scent of your father's cologne
so that when you leave, you can still find him
in the bottom shelf of the store
a reminder that a memory is where the mind and body connect.

Your body, ever changing, but still remembering its roots
a wondrous case for all that is you on the inside
Your body, a reminder that there is no such thing
as anything perfect,

just something in need of love, and reminders,
and words of affirmation to grow and heal.
to survive and thrive.

TENDER

Your spine curves
to fit the empty space in front of my body.
My arm wraps around you from behind you.
You reach for my wrists gently,
pull me closer.
I de-fist my hands
and let go of all that keeps me up at night.
Here with you,
I fit my fingers into the spaces
in between your long rough fingers.
They become soft.
and it is here that I feel like I am melting.
I do not want time to pass.
Everything feels still.
I am holding the thousands of stories that hide under your skin.
I must be one of them.
This is my peace, my slice of heaven.
on your make-shift small bed
that you have outgrown, meant for one, here we are.
We find ourselves quietly resting our bones,
one body curving to fit the silhouette of the other.
Hold me.
Here, there is no one to answer to.
We whisper *do not disturb* into the night
Bodies speaking without saying a word.
But here, you know I got you.
I know how you crave to be held.
I know how you crave to be soft.
You do not have to tell me.
I hold you because the world outside cannot fit you in its arms.
You are hard to digest, so you toughen your skin.

It becomes thicker and thicker except when you are here. with me.
I know it because this is my story, too.
We are both made to be that which we are not.
If this right here is our safe space,
let it be the softest space.
Let this be our peace.
Let this be everything still.
Our bed peace.

TOMBSTONE

This one's for you,
the one who opened these covers
to search for your reflection in these pages.
Rest now
You have arrived.

Your eyes are heavy
from scanning these pages for my hate poem
or the one where I mention the way
I vehemently despise all that you are
and the love that you wasted.

But dear, you will find
that only love lives here today,
even underneath the pain poems
embedded in the stanzas of sin.
You will only find yourself
in the words you choose to jump into.
If the poem fits, take it.

I will burn the idea of turning our story
into any beautiful mosaic of words.
I will spit out your vile venom
and sweep all the pieces of me you broke
right to the side so that I can breathe free
and make sense of this tragedy.

I will fall into the arms of new loves
and your memory will fade slowly but surely.
I will let you arrive and leave like the raindrops

Pitter

        Pattering

              On

                    My

                        Windowsill

                            Flowing

                              Downwards

                                  Naturally

                        Until you float away

Here, you will find the poem that lays you to rest.

I am

    letting   you   go.

                                  I am choosing

  my

own   winding   curving   road.

Close these covers.

Put

  me   down.

and rest assured that your love does not live here anymore.

DEVIL IN THE RED STILETTOS

She finds you in the nighttime.
4 a.m. anxiety plagued minds
are her favorite to consume.

You try to lay *doubt* to rest in her own casket.
She finds the *what* ifs from your headspace,
picks and plucks at the *should haves* like thorns.

hands them a platform, puts second guessing on its own stage,
provides imposter syndrome its own mic.
She amplifies the words of those around you,
the ones that don't quite understand your path, yet.

You protest her, hunt her down,
tracing the echoes, you hear from her voice.
You go in for the kill. She isn't an easy thing to prey on–,
isn't an easy thing to defeat.

At some point she carves her way out of her own tombstone,
haunts you when you least need her,
crowns you the black sheep, others you.
She mindfucks you until you come to the conclusion
that there is no way she can be right.

You have spent so many nights trying to prove her wrong,
hours losing sleep over trying to undo the choke hold she has on you,
nights trying to escape from her stiletto heel on your throat.

Her essence finds its way into your ears

even when you have tried to silence her,
or tried to extinct her. There comes a night,
it may be later than sooner, but the night arrives.
When the love you have within your body for yourself
spreads as a contagious virus that contaminates her blood,

she weeps, she is ill. Dying.
You are alive.

She shrinks every time you remind her of your own worth,
shrivels every time you machete her skin with your truth.
In this part, you look your demons in the face, and you know of their names.
You learn their habits.
You bury them with reminders of who you are,
what you will be, and how more than enough you already are.

Your demons haunt you
but you learn how to not let them swallow you whole.
This is how you survive.

You learn how to drown out doubt's voice,
which means you are to learn her scream
in the darkest hour of the night.
Hear it from afar, find the ropes
and refuse to let her sink you.

BLARING LOUD

Ain't she a bitch?
See how she struts in here all uninvited, staying here way too late?
Ain't anxiety *that* bitch?
The first one to arrive to the party and the last one to leave.

Ain't she a little too loud?
See how she walks in here telling me the things I already know?
Ain't she overprotective?

Doesn't she always have something to say?

She is never the last laugh, but rather the cliffhanger,
strutting out of the door leaving you wondering how to answer her back.

I want to tell her to leave, but I'm afraid she might take it the wrong way like,

What if she gets offended???
What if I fucked it up?!
What if I end up saying it all wrong?????   Or
Not saying what I *actually* mean.
What if my words get **stuck** at the back of my throat? What if?!
      What if this doesn't work out?
What if I am TOO much?

What if they *never* call?
What if they were *right*?
What if I was right?

Anxiety searches for all the what ifs, what abouts,
could haves and should haves from the inner corners of my mind.
It stitches them all together,
presses its weight down on my shoulders like bricks

Anxiety finds me when my mind is most still, seeps into my system, disrupts the silence, remains invisible, throws a party with all my demons. It will not hesitate to cling onto me like a child tugging at my feet, serves me self-doubt, shame, and second guessing all on the same plate. She is the last glance before the trust fall, the last steps before the jump. She is always the last word and without a doubt the first afterthought.

She has already made a comfortable home in my mind,
sets the bed after leaving it a mess the night before only to return.
She will ask 1,000 *why??*s
before any one sufficient answer crawls its way out of my throat.
She is the one who will keep me up at night and the first alarm in the morning.

Anxiety is like no other lover.
She leaves her home and finds her way to mine on demand.
She is loyal, unapologetic in her being,
will drag you after breaking you down
then challenges you all at once.

She keeps the door half open like there is always more of her to come, lets me know she isn't finished here yet,
holds me close to her.

Anxiety is my last reminder
that if I have survived her

and the many nights she has stolen from me
then I have survived all that has been out to get me
and all that is out to protect me at the same time.

I have survived all that has broken me into a million pieces by moonlight and all that has tried to stop me from putting it all together by sunrise.

LUST

Most days I cannot sit still.
I do not know what to do with the free time.
I crave too much flesh and feel too much hunger.

Thirsting while hydrated and feening while full,
always on the hunt. Too much night owl in my bones,
too lusty, a little too ready. Feral, ready to pounce,
ready to be unlocked, solved, to be feasted on, but not to be kept.

Most days I cannot understand myself, much less deal.
There are far too many growls coming from my stomach,
teeth too ready to sink into someone's neck.
Tongue too eager to taste your truth.

Wandering, wandering, looking, trembling, wandering, hoping.
Not lost, but ready to be found
Looking, hoping, showing up, dropping black lace to floor.
Jumping out of my own skin.

BE

They tell you that if you have ever deeply loved someone,
then you must let them go;
you must let them run wild.

In our case,
Put all the love you have ever had for me in a suitcase,
neatly packed.
Throw it over the river.
Pretend to start from scratch.

Be free, or freer.
Go far, like you have always been.
Book a hotel room or a cabin in the mountains or a flight across seas.

Go. Love her wildly. Watch it bloom.
Do all the things you didn't think you could with my hand in yours.
Be. Just be.
Give her hope.

I wish you moments you cannot turn your eyes away from.
I pray, how I pray you feel it in your bones,
shiver from the withdrawal.

I wish you a love that makes you feel alive again.
I know how you have withered from the inside for so long now.
I wish you safety.
I hope you feel what I felt so that you know.
I hope you find home in two arms

because it is all medicine.

Take a blanket with you
big enough to wrap two bodies in it.
I wish you warmth.
I pray you appreciate it.

I hope she smiles at you
and you believe it
and that your heart is ready.

Finally.

ONLY THING CHANGED WAS THE BLOCK

I dreamt last night that we were 12 years into the future
You and I met at a coffee shop on my block,
one that we had been to before.
You still remembered my order.
I still remembered your scent.

The block got a little more gentrified,
this time of the year a little colder.
The pothole in the road finally closed.
Your smile, still a complement to your laugh
still finds its way from your belly to comfort my bad jokes.

It had been years.
We only spoke on birthdays, and only missed some.
days where congratulations were in order,
snippets of your voice echoed over phone lines.
Every year, my one five-minute return to one of my first homes.

And there we were.
We decided it was time to sit across one another.
We were ready to be in one another's' presence
without fear of withering into a darker place,
without knowing which road this conversation may lead us down.
just here, to tell each other of the lifetimes that had crossed in these years

And still be able to breathe.

So, we did.

WORD VOMIT FOR THE MAN IN MY DM'S

In a DM on Instagram,
after I tell him "no thank you" he tells me
"You need to learn more about love,"

In this moment,
my words want to force themselves out of my belly past my
throat and onto this goddamn phone screen to let him know/ *All
I know is what it is like to live in love/ Or live in the absence of
love/*

But my fingers stop./ I know that he does not deserve all of
the words that have survived the quicksand./ Doesn't need any
justification/ my mind starts downward spiraling and every
moment in which love has swallowed me whole comes charging
at me like a rush to the head./ Like a bull fight/ If I could let him
know how many times I have been lost and found and lost and
found over and over and over/ Like a fever./ Would he get it?/ All
of the nights in which I loved like waves/ or soared through it or
drowned in it or broke because of it or/ picked myself up because
of it or picked myself apart because of it or let someone else's
wolverine nails tear through my love so conveniently/ or sur-
vived/ or found home in the way my first love held me through
three years of shelter/ Or the last time the foundation fell.

Or should I tell him of the time I was sold a false perception of
love, a narrative of fake promises and sweet whispers, only to
force the love out of me on a whiskey filled mattress. What about
the time I survived the unwanted grope of a thigh on a subway
train the first time or when a two- step to my favorite song on a
Saturday night at my favorite bar turned into a grab at the waist

and the thrust of the hip into a grind with an unsigned permission slip to get into these jeans. Or the night in which too much tequila was the reason he told me I deserved it. Doesn't every woman know of a "You asked for it" moment? Ain't this far too common?/Baby/If you knew what I knew because of what love taught me/you would not see this "no" as a jab to your stomach. You would see this rejection as a testament to this breath that has still kept this body alive even when love felt like an icepick to the skin/Or when it came in the form of a man who cried wolf, then became wolf./How quickly sugar turned into salt then rubbed into the wound/How quickly I turned into a lion.

Dear rejected lover in my Instagram DM, do you want to know of the time love shook my core enough to break me apart and tear this vessel of a still surviving body open to find what was still there? A heartbeat/If you saw rejection as information rather than a sting to the skin and that not every woman wants love to knock at her doorstep. Maybe this time all she wants is to fall so deep into herself that every crack in her skin, or tear or wound heals itself. Maybe all she wants is the time lost to rewrite itself, to rewrite this history./Maybe this is what they mean by she is reclaiming her time. Maybe the no just means no temporarily, a brb. Maybe it has nothing to do with you. Maybe it is an "under construction", but never broken to be considered under repair. Did you know that being alone can still taste sweet, can still reap the same fruits, can still find the same honey taste of life even if there are no arms to protect her? When she isn't looking for love when she would rather hold off. Believe her when she says she isn't interested. It isn't always a reflection of what your love has to offer. Trust me, I believe you.

Take this no as a reflection of the love that grew through the cracks like roses, picked off one by one for her rather than given by someone else. That rejection doesn't mean you don't have anything to offer her, just that it means she got more to offer herself. Yes, she can still buy herself the flowers this time. Maybe on this shittier end of the stick there is more peace to inhale/Maybe this isn't the bitter end of the stick after all. Maybe this time you will take my no for what it is/a heavily armed guard at the gate/a no trespassing or loitering or waste my time kind of no/This no is the one she has scraped from under the rubble, so know this.

Maybe this time, my no sounds sweeter because it found its rhythm again, danced its way off of my tongue on its own, by its own.
It finds its way out through the crack in between my lips, signed, sealed and delivered to you with a pretty little stamp.

But no return address this time.

MISSED CALLS

I have a bad habit of not listening even when I should.
I reek of rebel most days
I am just trying to stay afloat.

I admit that I should have known to stay anchored
because I should have seen it coming.
You see, I know I know better.
My gut feeling calls, and I do not answer.

She leaves as many missed calls as needed
in order to get the point across.
My intuition leaves voicemails,
but I do not open them,
no matter how strong this vibration is,
how loud my protectors scream
or how brightly my guardian angels
try to light my way.

Sometimes I choose what I know will not serve me well
because I am tired of abiding by the rules.

I do not know how to admit to being at fault.
I've got too much pride.
No matter the size of the aching pit in my stomach
that is itching at my insides trying to get a message across,
telling me what I know and what I need to do
and how I need to do it,
I choose ignorance because they tell me ignorance is bliss
and I need bliss just as much as I need peace over this noise.

I know I have bad habits.
I let things slide when I should have stopped them in their path.
I know I choose to walk boldly into trouble,
always loved the way the orange meets the blue
in the flames of the fire
I know not to get scorched by this heat.

I would rather hide than to be seen,
than to know that there is something out there or in me
that knows me better than I do.
My gut feelings know me better than I do, and I hide,
which is to say I know how to hide from truth
Which is to say that sometimes,
there is more light and comfort in the shade.
Some days I do not want to learn,
do not want to heal or grow
do not want to be the best version I know I can be.
Some days I just want to be.

But I know that my intuitive feelings are handed to me
by an army of ancestors going to war trying to protect me.
Yet, I close my ears.
I let trouble consume me because some days my excuses yell louder than my gut.
Some days, "just because" feels more of a reason, more than an excuse.
Some days my bad decisions win.

But today,
I honed in.
I listened in.
I put my ego down in a softer place.

I put all the impulsivity in a corner
neatly tucked away to make room for the stillness.

My gut called again. I answered.
She told me she would always return
no matter how much I ignored her.
She holds me.

My intuition reminds me that I know myself better
than I think I do,
that sometimes I just need to listen.

THIS COUNTRY IS CAGING OUR CHILDREN

There are children in cages.

There are children in

    cages.

There are
children in c a g e s.

The year is 2021 and there are children in CAGES.

There are children in cages.

There are children in cages
and boys behind bars and women holding scars in their skin.

Kids in detention instead of meditation.
Numbers assigned to lives
Shrunk down to digits,
school courtyards that look more like prisons than playgrounds

Children in cages and foil blankets for warmth
and cement floors for beds.
Newborns ripped from their mothers
in the honor of red and blue
Tell me why all I can see is red. all I can feel is blue.

In this country we are feeding our children competition instead of consciousness.
We shove white washed curriculums down the throats of brown students

once sitting in chairs that you and I once sat in.

It makes me think, how much white did I need to wash out of my own system
to embrace the brown that seeped through the cracks
yearning to be loved?
How much talent did we standardize
in the name of admittances to Ivy league institutions
that would rather give us a seat without letting us speak
than to feed us what we crave and see us fly?

They tell Amerikkka to celebrate
by setting off fireworks of red and blue,
run sirens across hoods shining lights of red and blue,
split people into half and ask them to be loyal to red and blue
crippling bodies with blood dripping down wounded legs
in wars to protect red and blue.
Amerikkka must be hot and cold at the same time.

Amerikkka tells my students to cut themselves into pieces
that are digestible enough,
tells them they are not enough
before telling them, they are too much.

She cuts locs, bans hijabs,
stops the student who is falling asleep in the front row,
gives him a number, puts him in detention
to become yet another statistic.

My children are locked in a system that will tell them how to sit,
and how to stop spreading their wings.
When wings were meant to soar.

THE FIRST CITY THAT STOLE YOU

I remember Toronto.
You said every street was a grid, easy to get around.

You said we could find our way back to each other
if we lost our way.
We learned the roadmap quickly.
You never wanted to leave.
You said there was something in the air that felt right.

I remember Toronto.
How I didn't want you to be far.
How our favorite city became the first threat,
a deportation back to yourself.
How I was jealous of the way she captured you enough.
How I was in love with her too
but hated the way she threatened to take you from me.
How you so easily considered making her a permanent part of your story
over a half week span and took years to see the same in me.

You loved this city and that city boldly too,
so I told you to go for it, to chase your dreams wildly
because I loved you, I needed you to fly,
need to see the soul in your smile. I lived for this.

I told myself I would fit myself into your life
no matter which city stole you from me.
I crowned myself necessary,
etched myself into your narrative only to be proofread later.
Erased, how you can still see the mark.

The imprint on the page, the rubber pieces shredding paper.
A hole now.

I always told myself that I was yours enough
for you to figure it out.
I titled myself as worthy.
I named myself permanent.
I put you on a throne.
Important enough for me to figure out
how to take you with me everywhere.

This wasn't the first threat of distance, the first time you left.
I remember the gaping hole that burned itself into my belly.
How you told me not to worry.
How you told me you would see me again.
How when I did, an empty gaping pit closed.

How you made me whole.
How you made me full.
How this was the fault in our story the entire time.

HENNESSY BLUES

I used to mask my rage with Hennessey.
When you left, the anger seeped its way into my system,
infused itself into my bloodstream,
gave me permission to lose myself.

Becoming friends with the bartender became the hobby,
a talent. a reminder that I wasn't completely numb yet,
but that I was on the way to being so.

The affinity for liquor never ran in my lineage,
never showed up as some form of trauma passed down to me
from my father or grandfather.
I served it to myself straight no chaser.

I wrote myself a false narrative, justified this over and over.
Bottles piling up one by one on the kitchen counter like trophies.
Glass art, forming a gallery walk of bad decisions,
an array of vices that I could pick from.
Both the poison and the medicine, the survival and the coping

You being ripped from me,
left me with a bitter taste in my mouth.
an excuse to cover up the root of the issue,
a denial of this new reality, a suppression of this past,
a consistent and persistent search
for a feeling that I could not name,
A supplement to drown the fear.

The bottle was the solution to the solitude,
a lullaby for the insomnia,

the bodega man with his open doors
being the only man I grew to trust.
The little girl inside me pleaded to be heard,
put her hands together, fingers embellished in rosary beads
wanting me to put the glass down and pick up the holy water.
Her cries for help, an eerie reminder
of how much I had let her down
and how deeply she wanted me back.

On the days where she screamed for help
and begged for my attention,
tugged at the rope to bring me back to shore,
I let go of it and told her I would swim back when I was ready.
I refused the life jacket, chose the drowning again,
fed myself excuses through the vessel of the shot glass,

The resurrection came in bits and pieces,
mostly remnants of myself that were still there.
I was put back piece by piece,

The moon found her way to peep through the windowsills
past the wine glasses.
She put her gentle hands on my wounds
even when they were still bleeding
and gently sang me to sleep.

People who embody pieces of my heart,
who knew exactly what to say without saying it,
lines of missed calls one by one answered,
only to remind myself of the life I built outside of this,
outside of you.

They never told me to put down the cup.

It never was about the messenger.
That just because there is destruction
doesn't mean that everything is completely broken
That yes, you can still rebuild.
After all, empty buildings make for the best fixer uppers.

I gave myself the second chance,
dug my way out from six feet under,
painted the bottles and filled them with flowers,
threw a few of them away, purged out a second life.

I knew I had recovered when finally,
finally, the drinks stopped pouring because of the memory of you.
But rather a clinking of glasses in honor
of all that I had built around me from the rubble.

SINK

On the days where the world weighs heavier than you can bear
on your two shoulders, lift it off and lay it down.

On the days where your words are swallowed, not written,
let them sink into you.

On the nights where lovers leave instead of staying,
hold the door open and let the night love you whole.

On the days where you feel far from home or far from yourself,
take one step. That is all.

On the days where the sunrise feels more like a choke than a wake,
let the sun speak, inhale the air.

On the days where you feel like you are a burden as much as you
may know you are not,
offer only love in your inhale and gratitude in your exhale.

On the nights where the stars do not align perfectly,
remember your voice, a vessel for the words that sink into others'
veins.

Remember the blessing it is to heal and break
and heal and break and heal and break all over again.

And which muscle can relate better than the heart?

What I am saying is that you are a whole heart.

Accept nothing less than the messages that tell you this very truth. and remember that home is in your hands.

And that you, my dear friend

are poetry.

OUTRO

Do not call it a funeral.
do not dare call it the saddest day you lived to see.
Do not staple my headshot onto a corny,
cursive letter lined invitation.
No. My passing will be a **goddamn celebration**.

Wear your colors.
Please, lord wear your colors.
No all black everything, unless you decide to make it look fly.
Bring your flowers but bring your Hennessey too.

Tell my best friend to take the aux cord
and attach it to the speakers we would blast our favorites from.
She knows exactly what I could shake and move to
and belt out loud in my bathroom, shower or car.

Bump that Biggie or Pac,
Some Nas, Lauryn Hill, Drake and Meg, too.

Make it a VIP Coachella type of deal
with only my closest friends and family, too.
Make 'em all dance, jiggle and sway their hips like I used to.

Invite all of my loves, exes, lovers, crushes, and everyone in between.
Tell them to share their favorite memories of me.
Whisper into the heavens how fast the tears dropped from their faces. I need to know.

When my body lays in its casket,

make sure that wood is iced out
with diamonds and sapphires.
Hell, throw my crystals in there, too.
Graffiti the walls, let me ride out in style.
No depressing black cars leading the procession
unless they are led by a block party
riding all the way through the city
to take me wherever they need to.

Light the Kush, take the shots, do not think about
what tomorrow may bring.

Bury me with my poems,
so that should you cremate me,
my ashes get fused with my art.
In fact, take my ashes.
Tell my three children to spread them across the ocean
right near my favorite little viewpoint down by RPV.
Breathe my words into the sunset.
Let it remind you of the full life I have lived.
Play my pictures on a slideshow,
laugh at the more embarrassing ones
Let my friends tell you of my deepest secrets,
the ones infused with too much tequila.
I'll let them make fun of me one last time.

Lastly, go into my side drawer table
and bring with you to my funeral
every picture, greeting card and letter I have ever saved.
Find everyone in them
make a collage around a tree,
etch your most cherished memory of me into the trunk
and let my essence live on in this Earth.

Let my death be known
as the greatest gathering you ever went to
and the greatest reminder of how loved you are.

Petals

ON DYING. AND LIVING

You tell me I am too young to think about death,
that twenty-seven is no time for me to think about the end.

I'll tell you this.

If I am not constantly thinking about the day I part from this Earth
or the way in which this body will transition
or how tomorrow is not promised,
then I truly do not know how to live fully in my time here.

My mortality is the compass to finding light.
My death is not the darkness.
My mortality makes all of the living seem like
the only thing worth doing in this physical realm.

STRAIGHTENED AND SCORCHED

I have spent so many years
trying to straighten out the kinks in my hair.
The waves, curls and frizz, the fly-aways and baby hairs
The years of heat damage made the hair start to break and fall.

The years of scorching my own blessings.
the amount of time spent every morning
trying to hide what made me, me.

The problem all along was the way the white world saw my hair
as untamed, messy, hard to control, out of control, like a jungle.
These things were never meant to be hidden.

My waves and curls are the protest.
A visible statement saying, "Fuck you."
It is a rebuttal to fight back that took years to embrace.
Years to stop burning alive what makes me beautiful.

CRESCENT

Maybe I am too much golden hour sunset for you to inhale,
too much moonlight for you to exhale.
Too much. Too much. Too much.

If this is the case, leave the door open,
slightly ajar when you leave
so that a lover born from sunrise may find me,
envelop my skin with their warmth

and hold me until I am asleep
under only the shine of the stars
and the promise of morning.
Like the moon, I know I deserve the morning
just as much as I needed the night.

SIP

Give me:
a love like fine wine.
Better with age, robust, flavorful,
wisdom soaked in sweetness,
luscious, slow intoxication
uncorked, spilled
tangy enough to leave you wanting more
something tasted on the lips,
aromatic, ever changing.
best appreciated through a slow sip
soaked into taste buds
picked from the finest shelf.
Bottled up carefully
only to be opened by those with a craving for it,
those with an affinity for it,
never second guessing its complexity,
but rather expecting layers
anything but unforgettable.
Leaves you wondering how something so complicated
was made to glide through the tongue so smoothly.

TRUST FALL

Loving you was like:
you convincing me that the trust fall would be fun
and worth it and everything I needed
to feel the wind in my bones again.

You spun me around
while I got dizzier and dizzier,
held my body in place,
moved the hair out of my face with your soft fingers.

You told me to lose my balance,
so I did. I let go
and found nothing to catch my fall.

ILLUSION

My wish for you is that you do not tremble
when your first love haunts your new love.
That you do not sink when you find pieces of them in the way
your new love holds you.

That you do not fall victim to an illusion,
because old lovers will always, always travel through new ones,
but they will not stay. My wish is that you will greet them,
thank them for showing up, and still fall in your new love's arms
because home may be of the same concrete,
but never of the same frames on the walls
Never the same coat of paint, never the same fireplace,

and maybe love will challenge you
to bear witness to ghosts,
Let them float.
Let your heart unwind
and fall into the new arms
you have fought for
that you deserve.

Isn't it something?

that the moments in which there is a
complete loss of words

are the same moments in which poems
full of words are born

villages can be born from emptiness.

SPOONFUL OF HONEY

L   o   v   e

is the longest four-letter word I have ever learned.
It has taken me years to fully taste its meaning on my tongue,
to savor it whole. Multiple loves to digest it.
Punches to the gut over and over to understand its depth
and many nights to give me the meaning of it, raw and pure.

BARRED

When did we start to cage our love?
Put it behind bars when it kept asking to be fed
and only let it out at times diced it in half,
giving it to each other in increments.

When did it become okay to serve love an injustice?
To strip it away when we needed it the most?
When did it ask us to tarnish it?
When did we stop fighting for its survival?

How did we come to terms with gifting it to each other
half wrapped and split into parts?

Haven't we learned that love's body is fluid?
Comes running back to us even when wounded,
sits ready at our doorstep even when we don't let it in.

When will we finally get that love shows no mercy
for those with their fists up,
still wins the fight every time.

The truth is this:

The pen has saved me more times than I remember
Spilling ink was always better than spilling my own blood.

MY GRANDMOTHER BEFORE SHE BECAME A GRANDMOTHER

My grandmother was a woman of her own story before my
grandfather became a part of hers.
My mother was her own woman of dreams, red lipstick,
fireworks and honey dripping in her footsteps
far before my father walked her way.
If this truth has taught me anything, it is this:
that my daughter and her daughter must learn that
I was a multiverse before any man put a ring on it.
They must know my anthology before they know my sequels.

You do not need to earn anyone's love.
You do not need to earn anyone's love.
You do not need to earn anyone's love.
You do not need to earn anyone's love.
You do not need to earn anyone's love.

THROAT CHAKRA

I do not have to know you for a lifetime to love you.
I have loved you since we met.
I have an abundance of it in my heart,
plenty of it in my body
an ocean of it in my mind,

just a shortage of it in my throat.

SACRED

With or without you, in your presence or not,
I am still the most sacred version of myself there is,
still magnificently whole.

No matter how much I feel nourished
from you watering my petals,
no matter how much I crave what you feed me.

Regardless of the growth within me I feel
from being with you
I must, I must, I must remember this truth:
I have been surviving and will continue to survive.

There is a garden around me that loves me whole
for my leaves and for my thorns.
and no part of you will change this.

You may stay or you may leave,
but the sun will always choose me in the morning
and will always greet me with a kiss on the cheek.

BITTERSWEET

I would imagine/that the part you will miss the most about me/is the adoration that I had for you/unfiltered, pure wholesome bliss/how it spilled all over you/slowly but sweetly, and organically/like honey/There is no going back/You will try to find this texture in every lover/In every person that shares space with your body/ But you will end up lost/you will not find the exact same flavor of this nectar anywhere/nor the same shade of hazel/nor the exact same sweetness on the tongue/

This is why they call it bittersweet when I go.

THE CLOSING

Find a stack in the library to tuck away the memory.
Look for the right floor, section, genre, code on the right shelf.
Ask the librarian to help you,
with her two wrinkled hands reeking of wisdom.
Close the covers and glide the collection
to fit into just the right gap.
Fill the void and call it closure.
Don't judge the book by the cover
even when it has been returned too early.
Remove the bookmarks left from the previous reader.
White out the places where the pen left its marks.
Get band aids for the paper cuts
Let new fingers swim across the corners.

EVOLUTION

When I love myself
and my hips be swinging just a lil' too extra
and the wind hits my hair in a way that breaks necks
and the world stops to witness this evolution
and the moon cycles don't even make me flinch

it is then that I feel the heat of my own body.
I return home to what was always mines
finally

but here I am, livid.
that the road map to how I got here
was *you*.

TWENTY SEVEN

I have lived three lifetimes in this one.
Three eras in 27 years.

Which means that there are only three things I know to be true.

There was a life before your arrival.
In this one, I was lost.

There was a life when you arrived and stayed.
In this one, I was found.

There is a life after you left.
In this one I am found over and over again.

In this one, I learn every day,
that your departure was always the road home.

Never the drowning.

Pollen

FLOW

If we could grow flowers instead of blades
from all of the moments we have survived,
the garden I would nurture for you
would birth more air to breathe.
colorful dainty reminders
of all that has not got the best of you,
petals flowing in the wind,
free and able to flow wherever this all takes you.
Soil as fertile with wisdom
as the wrinkles in our grandmothers' cracked tooth smiles.

My goodness, if we could birth gardens and flowers
instead of blades, become softer instead of steel,
become water instead of ice.
If we could share more instead of holding it in,
release instead of retreat,
look our demons in the face and say
you will not take me today.
How we would not be afraid of waves.
How we would let go of fear as freely as our love goes into the wind.

If we could grow simpler, not more complicated
from all that has tried to get us.
How this world would feel more Pisces flow
than the sting of a Scorpion every time.
How we would float if we found light in the struggle.
How we would let it carry us through the elements.

How our seeds would be replanted here and there
because maybe that is the process,

maybe healing is the win and not the burden.
How we can choose to say,
This right here will not steal me
from the rest of this life there is yet to live.

How we would strut through fire.
How we would see that we are all broken things together
but how all we need is a little water and sunlight to help us grow.
Do you not see how the moon falls every night and the sun still,
still finds a way to wake you in the morning–
plants a kiss on your cheek and whispers to you, "Try again."

How we would see that sinking a bit doesn't mean drowning,
it just means there is more to learn
from that which has swept us under
like the tide that tried to get you
Or a tsunami at times.

How we would love the ocean whole
even if it swallows us deep
because somewhere anchored to the ocean floor
there is still something growing, still sprouting,
close to its roots still deserving of love
for all that she has survived.

Even if she is at the bottom,
she still has quite the view, doesn't she?
still has a story to paint from the deeper shades of blue,
from all that has tried to tear her from her roots.

but fails.

THE GIFT OF THE SUNFLOWER

The yellow sunflower faces upwards in the sky,
follows the sun as her stem strengthens.
Sometimes she wilts when she hasn't been nourished.

You call this half ass,
weak, easy, too noticeable.
that to be a flower means
that I can still be easily covered
by the weeds around me.

You say, a flower should rise to the occasion stand tall.

You expect the flower to be the tree,
to weather the same storms in the same way
and still stand firm and stay in the same place.

You tell me one should never be so fragile enough
to be picked so swiftly, to be folded or dismissed
or thrown into the wind
that one should never be at the disposal
of the strong fingers of trespassers,
who selfishly pick apart the flower's skin

You call the sunflower meek.
You do not know I am one.
That you are the trespasser.

I tell you the gift of the sunflower is this:
That no matter it's fragile stem,
no matter how dainty she appears,

no matter how close to the ground she stands,
sometimes shoulders wilted downwards,
She can still see the soil she comes from,
still thrives in it no matter how infiltrated it may be.

The tree that you are is withered bark
is chipped, is spoiled roots, ready for war on the outside
poisoned by toxicity on the inside,
not because of age, not because you have been used,
climbed upon; or limbs broken here and there.

It is because those who look down on the flowers
that come from the same Earth & the same soil
will never grow as strong as you claim to be.

Those who see the flower as less important,
less powerful, will always forget their roots
no matter how firm they may be.
These are the ones who will always be lost.
No matter how tall, no matter how tough on the outside,
no matter how much closer to the sun you may seem to feel.

SPINE
(for you)

You could have been anywhere,
but you choose to graze the spine
that holds together the pieces of me.
You uncover a labor of love,
heartbeats sewn into the fabric of these pages.

You could have been in the company of your most beloved,
but you choose to meditate on words
that I carefully constructed for you, for us.
Polaroid snapshots of my love,
a collection of feelings stitched together
to form a piece of me in your hands.

You could have been anywhere,
but you chose me, my words and my poetry.
Maybe you found pieces of yourself in these stanzas.
If so, welcome home.

You hold my layers in your hands.
You infuse the sound of my voice into your ears.
You find a way to hear the cracked voice
in the parts that have hurt the most.
or maybe you fill these words
with a backdrop of your own voice
because maybe you want to reclaim this as your story, too.

You take this time to be gentle.
You acknowledge me.
You read between the lines.

You adopt the metaphors and similes
that encompass parts of your own plot
and I tell you to take them, feel them,
love them as if they were your own.
You do.

You find missing syllables you thought went astray,
only to find that what you see in my lines
are just mere reflections of the best parts of you,
flaws and all.

And you gently,
close the back cover with a sigh with love,
as you breathe through these last few words.
You must feel one more thing.
My gratitude for you, for our worlds colliding
and for my art to be held by you.

After all, you are the only set of eyes
and the only pair of hands
that I would ever let consume me whole like this.

This is not a parting.
This is you carrying the best parts of me,
after the worst parts tried to get me.

This is you and I meeting at the crossroads of our survival.

RAVINA WADHWANI

is a Los Angeles based poet, mental health therapist, advocate and educator who made her way to the West Coast by way of the East Coast. Ravina was born and raised in the U.S. Virgin Islands and embraces her South Asian roots and multicultural upbringing. She is a first-generation South Asian American woman who uses writing as a tool for understanding identity, processing trauma, moving through experiences of struggle, empowerment, growth, joy and healing. Ravina credits her family's immigration history as the catalyst for experiencing the world, and finding multiple homes all over the Mother Earth. She honors and deeply cherishes the incredible chosen family she has made along the way. Ravina has lived in the U.S. Virgin Islands, the Canary Islands (Spain), the United Kingdom, Massachusetts and California. Ravina often reflects and hold space for processing issues existent in the South Asian diaspora. She is also a facilitator of trauma-informed healing circles for survivors of gender based violence and communities of color affected by systemic issues of oppression.

Yellow is her first collection of published poetry and prose. Ravina sees healing and art as a lifelong commitment and journey to honor the well-being and liberation of this generation and the generations that come after our time on Earth.

www.ingramcontent.com/pod-product-compliance
Lightning Source LLC
Chambersburg PA
CBHW031319160426
43196CB00007B/584